OUT
OF THE
RUINS

TINA TRAN

THOUGHT CATALOG Books

Copyright © 2016 by Tina Tran. All rights reserved. Published by
Thought Catalog Books, a publishing house based in Williamsburg,
Brooklyn and owned by The Thought & Expression Company *www.thought.is*.
This book was art directed by Chris Lavergne and Mark Kupasrimonkol.
Project management was handled by Alex Zulauf. Illustrations are by
Amanda Mocci. The digital version was built by KJ Parish.

For Kris - you will always live in
the margins of my poems.

MOMENTUM

I

The way your hand trembles slightly
as it searches for mine,
how my breath catches when
they finally meet-
all at once, every feeling
we've ever felt comes rushing towards us,
tidal waves of emotion.
It breaks us, reshapes us,
turns us into something new.
This is what love does to you.
Moments like these exist
to remind us what we live for.
We become light.
We become alive.

II

Teach me how to love you so good
our hearts will be beating
thunderously
against our ribcages
straining to get out.
For so long I have only known
how to hurt.
There are scars on my body like
constellations.
The one on my hip was from when I was six
and I learned my parents were
the Titanic and the iceberg.
My wrist has a faint bruise
reminding me of when I gave myself
to a boy who crashed and burned
and took me down with him.
Heartbreak sounds a lot like
a slamming door.
Show me it doesn't have to be this way,
I want to be proven wrong.
Teach me how to love right.

III

We created magic when we kissed.

IV

I fell for you the way a train
wrecks itself,
the way a wave crashes into the shore.
It looks like fear
and it feels like recklessness.
So maybe we'll destroy each other,
ruin and break each other
but God,
what a way to go.

V

I can't explain what it does to me
when your hands are on my skin.
My body is a landmine
and I'm itching
for an explosion to happen.

VI

I've split myself open for you.

VII

I hope
that if alternate universes exist,
it will still be you
and me
in the end. I hope that
there will always be an us.
In every world,
in every story.

VIII

You feel like a dream I never woke up from.

IX

1

Give me the sensual curves of your body,
where skin glides over bone so effortlessly.
You are a work of art that
historians would spend their whole life studying.

2

I want to play your body like a violin:
move my fingers so eagerly across the jut
of your hipbones,
croon my name so that it sounds
like a symphony is playing on the tip
of your tongue.

3

We are not like any lovers that the world
has ever seen before;
at night we resemble punctuation,
two parentheses and the space between us.

X

I'm next to you and miles exist
between us.
Will I always be the one
running after a train
I can never catch?
My hands itch to build a bridge
that could one day reach you.

XI

The world is spinning madly as
I pass by these frenzied strangers.
I hope you know
I look for you
in everyone.

XII

It's always been you. Every time.

XIII

If I tried to explain
how I felt,
it would be like shouting
into the sun.
What can I do?
I'm always waiting for her
to show me the side of her
no one else gets to see.
But like everyone else,
I'm sitting in the dark.

XIV

You are the one that waits.
You always have been,
ever since you were young enough
to believe in heroes and villains,
dragons and knights.
In your queen sized bed
that felt like an island,
you waited
every night for him to come.
You looked for his shadow.
Maybe this time it will be different.
So when the lights turned off
and the hallway went dark,
you turned your back to the door.

XV

It hurt, but I still stayed.

XVI

I want to relive every moment I had with you.
Even if it hurts.
I need to know that what we had was real.

XVII

You lose yourself loving catastrophic people.

XVIII

I think of you when the flowers bloom
because you had made me
come alive.

I think of you when the sun is out
because your brilliance had illuminated
even the darkest parts of me.

I think of you as the rain is pouring down
because your love was a storm
and I could never tell
if I was going to be
drenched in it
or end up thirsting for what I lacked.

I think of you on bitter winter nights
because I never felt as cold
as I did
when you left.

I think of you when the seasons change
because you did too.

XIX

We were strangers on a train
and then you said, 'Hello.'
We were friends
who shared stolen glances.
Your laughter became my favorite song.
We were lovers.
We created a new language
only our bodies knew how to speak.
We were comfortable.
The phone calls came less often.
Your clothes no longer littered my floor.
There was no wreckage,
no casualties.
We were just ships
passing in the night.

XX

People loved you and left scars.

LOSS

XXI

I hope you read this someday
and know
I fought like hell for you.

XXII

I loved you to the point of ruin.
I loved you until my lungs were filled with ash.

XXIII

My secrets hang around like warm breaths
on cold winter mornings.
Yours always lingered
on the roof of your mouth.
There used to be nights where I was tempted
to set myself on fire.
Would you remember me then?
You live in the margins of my poems now.
I only wanted to be yours,
I wanted to be yours.

XXIV

Tell me darling,
who stole the light from
your soul?
I see the way you hold yourself
so
tightly.
(Maybe you are afraid
you will float away.)
You are a building,
standing so tall
but a single word
would
demolish
you.

XXV

The worst thing about growing up
is realizing that you can't save anyone.
They are on a ship hit by an iceberg
and you are on the coast.
All you can do is love them from afar
and then you're forced to watch them either
sink or float.
That is why I bury my hurt
so deep that
you will never find it.
You already are weighed down by so much,
and the odds are already stacked
up against you.
I don't need to be the heavy in your life.

XXVI

I wanted to be your everything
more than I wanted to be my own
and that is why
I had to leave.

XXVII

I love you,

I love you.

But I can't keep sacrificing pieces of myself

to make you whole.

My heart is clenching like a fist

trying to get me to stay.

Leaving quietly,

moving on without looking back,

is not something

I know how to do.

XXVIII

We fell too hard and broke.

XXIX

When it comes to you,
I am a dandelion.
You hold me in your hands
and ask for more than I can give
and I,
I just fall apart.

XXX

6:15 AM: I start missing you when I leave in the morning.

6:15 PM: I'm still missing you when I come home to an empty house.

I spend all of my time trying to forget you in the space in between.

XXXI

I wrote novels about his absence.

XXXII

He said that he will love me better
than any man can.
He thinks he can save me,
that he could be my salvation,
my sun, my star, the light in my eyes.
But the truth is
I don't care to be rescued.
My solitude is a lover that
I will always return to.
And if he stays,
he will learn that I am
the anchor that will unmercifully drown him
in the sea.

XXXIII

Footsteps echo on the pavement.
I try to remember
what it was like
when you were walking towards me
instead of walking away.

XXXIV

I want to wash
your name from my
mouth
and
learn how to
sleep alone
again.

XXXV

In our sleep,
we're still happy.
We're still together.
Until I'm back in my dreams,
I'll continue to write about a love
that only exists in my memories.

XXXVI

Take long showers and scrub your skin raw
until it becomes red
and their touch has been washed off,
their kisses and caresses spiraling down the
drain.

Say their name over and over again,
until it becomes distorted
and foreign in your mouth,
so all that's left are traces of a bitter taste.
Wash it down with a glass of wine
or two
or three.

Remove all the sheets and covers
that were once entangled with their legs
and embedded with their scent.
Clean them. Rip them. Burn them.
Buy new ones. Buy a new bed,
one where the mattress has yet
to conform to their figure,
outlining their curves perfectly
and reminding you of all the sleepless nights
spent having conversations with their mind
and their body.

Start hating yourself
because no matter what steps you take
you can never forget them.
You don't even really want to.

XXXVII

There were 366 days this year.
I have spent each one of them missing you
and I will spend the next 365 doing the same
and the next,
and the next.

XXXVIII

Love is all about timing.
So maybe one day
we'll meet again
when we're different people.
Maybe then
we'll be better for each other.

XXXIX

In my head it was real.
In my head it felt so right.
But I opened my eyes
and you're not here
and it's just me
in my room
with empty hands
that were meant to hold you.

XL

So this is how to miss someone.
This is how to ache until
you forget how to be human.
There are no tears,
nothing but your breaths
breaking the silence in a
vacant room
and you realize
that your bed is too big
for just one person.

XLI

Hell is
loving you in my sleep
and waking up alone.

XLII

Either you want me around
or you don't.
I have no time to stick around for people
who are unsure of my worth.
If you miss me,
you should've known better than to let me
leave.

XLIII

I hear a small voice
in the back of my mind
and it is chanting a prayer:
'Please don't fall in love again,
please don't fall in love again.'
Maybe this time I will listen.
Maybe this time I will learn.

HEALING

XLIV

I once had an angel
who watched over my shoulder
and told me how to act like a lady.

When the boy with the threatening grin
pulled on my hair with his dirty hands
the angel stopped me from telling my mother.
Said, 'It's only because he likes you.'
So I kept quiet
and when the boy grabbed my wrist
hard enough to leave a bruise
I pretended it was instead
a birthmark conveniently formed
in the shape of a heart.

I was walking to work
when I heard a catcall from a car
stopped at a light.
I wanted to tell him that my existence
was not an open invitation to fuck me
but the angel told me
that I was overreacting,
so I smiled at him
while wishing the ground would
swallow me whole.

It was a Saturday night
and I was in bed
when he came tumbling into the room
smelling strongly of whiskey and cigarettes.
He pulled the covers off
and slid his hands up my thighs.
I told him I was tired but his hands
crept higher.
The angel told me to stay still,
to relish his touch
to make him feel good.
He wants you, let him have you.
So I listened and closed my eyes
and waited for it to end.

Later that night,
I sat on the bathroom floor
and carved into my skin
all the words the angel
has ever told me.

Be soft.

Do not raise your voice.

Cross your legs.

Smile.

Smile.

I once had an angel
who watched over my shoulder
and told me how to act like a lady
so I grabbed a .22
and shot it dead.
I had to kill my angel
before it killed me.

XLV

Tell me,
why do we continue to
teach our girls
to aspire to become nothing,
to fold into themselves
and swallow their voices?
Why do we tell them that
what we value most
is their negative space?

Daughters,
be loud
be brave.
Do not let yourself bleed anymore.
Take up space
until people can feel your power
from continents away.
Channel your rage,
your pain from being silenced
and make the world
tremble.
You are a force to be reckoned with.

XLVI

I am moving on without you.
No fanfare, no tears.
I'm packing my bags and
leaving silently.
It's the bravest thing I know how to do.

XLVII

Realizing I deserved better changed everything.

XLVIII

I always thought that I could never
live without you.
But it's been a few years
since I've heard your voice.
My hair is a lot shorter.
I sleep earlier than I used to.
I guess what I'm trying to say is
my world had fallen apart
and yet I am still here.

XLIX

Losing you made me find myself.

L

A year ago,
I used to be scared of being alone.
I had a habit of sitting next to strangers
on the bus
despite there being empty seats,
wrote my number on restaurant tables.
I sent drunk texts to my ex-lovers
hoping one of them would miss me too.
It will take you months, I learned,
before solitude grows on you.
Often, you will have to leave
before you are ready.
But it is worth waiting for.
One day, you will be able to say,
'This poem is not for you
and I am not sad.'

LI

I've been taught by my mother that love is another type of cancer. The kind that kills you slowly, by infecting your organs one by one until it turns your body against itself.

And maybe there is some truth in that. I grew up watching parts of my mother disappear with each and every lover, shrinking into herself like a wool sweater tumbling in the wash. That's why I let my spine stiffen, my tongue sharpen. I built myself a suit of armor made up of excuses and wore it every day.

Please don't come any closer. I'm fragile underneath. It's better for both of us if you leave.

But then came you. And piece by piece, I shed my armor.

I know you can hurt me, but I trust you not to. I don't want you to go. Please stay.

My mother would be surprised to see you and me together because instead of fading away, I become more of what I am meant to be.

I still hesitate when I say I love you because the words feel foreign in my mouth. Sometimes I don't call back because I forget that I have someone waiting for me at home. But I am learning.

So maybe love is neither the sickness nor the cure. Maybe love is simply the catalyst.

LII

The past won't ever defeat me.

LIII

You are the fire that courses through veins
and he tries to water you down.
Says he needs you,
can't live without you.
He clings to you like shackles
on your wrists; a beggar
who takes all that you have to offer
and still asks for more.
When you leave him (and you will),
as all strong girls like you
have done in the past,
he will cry for you to stay.
But you won't, will you?
(Independence is a cruel mistress.
I know this all too well.)
The world needs more girls like you-
fearless and burning brighter than the
dying stars that irradiate the night;
girls whose very presence
shatters
the universe a hundred times over.
Belonging to yourself is a custody battle
you will fight with all of the people you have
and will ever love.
I hope it's one you will let yourself win.

LIV

9 messages I left on your voicemail.

1 Do you still love me? Please call me back.

2 I found your shirt in my closet. It still smells like you. So do my bedsheets.

3 Last night, I woke up at 2 am and wrote in my journal the first thing that came into my head. I wrote that you are my phantom limb.

4 Someone told me I looked pretty today but all I could think about was what you were doing.

5 I scrubbed my skin until it turned pink because I can't fucking stand how I still feel your lips. I haven't left the house in days.

6 Drinking won't erase the memories. I've tried.

7 I looked in the mirror and couldn't find myself. I miss who I was before you.

8 Everything in the box belongs to you. I don't need it anymore.

9 My mother called and asked how I was doing. I said I went out to the store and bought milk. She told me she was proud of me. I hope you are too.

LV

I have made homes
out of so many people.
I used to never be able to
inhabit my own skin.
But now,
my body is a motel
and out on the lawn
there's a sign that flashes,
'No vacancy.'
The windows have cracks
and the floorboards squeak
and it is the most beautiful place
I have ever been.

LVI

Inside of you,
there's a little girl
and every night she cries.
Because of the way you talk to her
when you look in the mirror.
Because of the men
you let touch her.
Protect her. Love her. Be kind.
You are the only one
who can keep her safe.

LVII

Here is my apology
written on my wrist.
It says,
'Yes I've been to hell
and yet here I am.'
It will be the last
public apology I will ever make.
Who I am comes in waves.
If you're not careful
you might drown.

LVIII

One day, you will meet someone who will turn
your world
completely upside down.
You will feel vulnerable.
It might even be more terrifying than anything
else
you've ever experienced.
But you will also feel things that you have
never felt before,
things that you thought only existed in fairy
tales.

These people are worth waiting for. They are
worth everything.

LIX

My dear,

I know how lonely you get at times and how it feels like your ribcage is caving in.

It's tough, walking down the street and you see the lovers with their blushing cheeks trying to sneak a kiss. It's even worse at night when your thoughts have time to broadcast all of your insecurities.

But boyfriends and falling in love is not the end-all, be-all. I promise. You're only nineteen and you've only just begun to witness all that life has to offer. You are still a child of the earth.

You're going to graduate college, you're going to live out on your own, you're going to get a job you hate and you will get a job you love. You're going to travel and meet people. You're going to look into the mirror and see yourself the way you've always wanted people to see you. You're going to see sunsets and sunrises. You're going to celebrate birthdays and Christmases and Fourth of Julys. Having a boyfriend is wonderful but it's just one experience out of the many you will have.

Just wait, you will find someone one day with whom you can share all of these wonderful experiences that you've had and they're going to love you even more for it. Because your life does not begin and end with them.

LX

It's 1:24 a.m.
You're in your bed
wishing that someone would see your scars
as battle wounds. You were in
the fight of your life.
After all, how many people can say
with confidence,
that they are a living casualty?
(You killed the old part of yourself
that you thought no one could ever
love.)
Your Medal of Honor is an unopened bottle of
pills;
a glass of tequila that remains
untouched.
I am doing my best.
I am doing my best.
As if repeating that mantra
over
and over
would somehow make it true.
Please believe me when I say,
the leaves will change color
with the passing seasons. Sugar will taste sweet
when it runs down your tongue.

Like all those other truths,
you stand a little taller in space
without gravity weighing you down.
So let go of what plagues you.
Let yourself grow.
You'll be a little taller tomorrow.

LXI

I was twelve and you were my best friend. I talked to you under my covers because it was late and my parents had already told me to go to bed. It was the first time I stayed up past midnight talking to you, but it wouldn't be the last. When I hung up, you called me back because you forgot to wish me sweet dreams.

I was fourteen and you were my friend's older brother. I was crying because this was the first time I ever felt like my heart was completely cracked in two. You said that because my heart was broken, more love could be poured in than ever before. That one day, someone will spend every day trying to prove that they are good enough for me.

I was fifteen and you were the one I didn't see coming. We were strangers, who became friends. The first time we fought was when I knew I was in too deep. We were friends, who ended up becoming strangers.

I was eighteen and you were a quick fix. I was damaged and you were too. There was skin and desperate touches and whispered Oh God, you make me feel so alive. On one particular day, we were lying side by side. You turned to me and traced pictures on my spine. I sighed and you kissed me on the forehead. I never told you, but in that moment I had never felt more naked.

I am nineteen and air continues to fill my lungs. I belong to no one but myself. I am living without the shackles of my sadness. My heart beats because I see beauty and wonder. I see myself in the mirror and I think, this is what it feels like to be in love.

LXII

The first step to loving yourself
begins with the words,
'I matter.'
You deserve to occupy space.
You deserve to stand up for yourself
and claim your right to happiness.
You deserve to be here,
just as much as
anyone else.

LXIII

This year I am going
to shed my old skin.
I'm going emerge in a body
your fingers will not have touched.
I won't be yours anymore.
I will belong only to myself.

LXIV

Do everything to feel alive again.

LXV

There were always warning signs but you were blinded by hope and thoughts like, 'Maybe this time it'll be different'. You chose to stay inside a burning building until the smoke became too thick to clear and the foundation began to crack. But now it was time to get yourself out.

No one tells you, though, that trying to move on is a kind of death that you inflict upon yourself. People always make it sound so easy, as if by emptying the stuff in your house, you can empty yourself of the love you still feel.

The memories you have like to coddle you. Laughter and late nights drunk on the feeling of being young and infatuated. They deposited in you the way sand deposits onto wet summer skin. They stick on you in the most unconventional places, underneath fingernails and knobby knees. But you let them stay because it reminds you of how you were once in the water and the sun was beating on your neck.

You now know that was how you ruin yourself.

Before the word us turned into something singular, everything had already changed. You look back, really look back, and you see that he is not the same. And neither are you. So you release the fists clenching onto the past and you take off your rose-colored glasses.

You used to mistake the silhouette on the wall for yourself. Used to think of yourself as a stray cat scratching on his door, waiting to be let in again. Not anymore.

It takes time for you to realize that your life with him is not juxtaposed. It's not as simple as a before and after. He is just a detour on your journey. The destination is still there, waiting for you.

When you finally let go, it is like opening your front door and seeing yourself standing there again.

Welcome home, it's been so long.

LXVI

They don't tell you in school
how experience can teach you to heal
in all the wrong ways.
I sabotage myself so well,
bolt myself in
before others can open the doors.
My words are clumsy and awkward.
People regard me like a car accident;
they can't look away
from something so tragic.
Sometimes I forget how to be human.
I hope on those days,
you'd be willing to wait for me
to resurface.

LXVII

I'll wreck myself and begin anew.

ABOUT THE PUBLISHER

Thought Catalog Books is a publishing house owned by The Thought & Expression Company, an independent media group based in Brooklyn, NY. Founded in 2010, we are committed to facilitating thought and expression. We exist to help people become better communicators and listeners in order to engender a more exciting, attentive, and imaginative world.

Visit us on the web at www.thought.is or www.thoughtcatalog.com.

ABOUT THE WRITER

Tina Tran is a Tumblr poet and a curator of quotes. She writes to make others feel alive.

Find her online at absentions.net.